MW00533333

KETO DIET COOKBOOK
FOR WOMEN OVER 50

Make Your Body Work like it Used to, lose 15lbs in Just 3 Weeks with 32 Delicious Low Carb, Easy to Prepare Ketogenic Recipes for Senior Women to Regain Metabolism

© Copyright 2021 - All rights reserved.

The content contained within this book may not be reproduced, duplicated or transmitted without direct written permission from the author or the publisher. Under no circumstances will any blame or legal responsibility be held against the publisher, or author, for any damages, reparation, or monetary loss due to the information contained within this book. Either directly or indirectly.

Legal Notice:

This book is copyright protected. This book is only for personal use. You cannot amend, distribute, sell, use, quote or paraphrase any part, or the content within this book, without the consent of the author or publisher.

Disclaimer Notice:

Please note the information contained within this document is for educational and entertainment purposes only. All effort has been executed to present accurate, up to date, and reliable, complete information. No warranties of any kind are declared or implied. Readers acknowledge that the author is not engaging in the rendering of legal, financial, medical or professional advice. The content within this book has been derived from various sources. Please consult a licensed professional before attempting any techniques outlined in this book. By reading this document, the reader agrees that under no circumstances is the author responsible for any losses, direct or indirect, which are incurred as a result of the use of information contained within this document, including, but not limited to, errors, omissions, or inaccuracies.

Table of Contents

INTRODUCTION

Keto is a diet that requires cutting carbs and expanding fats to help the body consume its own fat stores all the more productively. Studies have shown that ketogenic diets are advantageous for in general wellbeing and getting more fit. Remarkably, ketogenic diets have helped certain individuals shed undesirable muscle to fat ratio without extraordinary desires that are regular of different diets. It's likewise been tracked down that a few groups with type 2 diabetes can utilize keto as an approach to control their manifestations.

How Ketogenic Diets Work

Ketones are at the focal point of the ketogenic diet. You can get thinner On Keto for Women. Over 50 your body produces ketones, a fuel particle, as an elective fuel source when the body is coming up short on glucose.

Creating ketones happens when you decrease carb allow and devour the perfect measure of protein.

At the point when you're eating keto well-disposed food varieties, your liver can move muscle versus fat into ketones, which at that point get utilized as a fuel source by your body.

At the point when the body is using fat for a fuel source, you're in ketosis. This permits the body to expand its fat consuming drastically now and again, which helps with lessening pockets of undesirable fat. Not exclusively does this technique for fat consuming assist you with getting in shape; however it can likewise avert yearnings and forestall energy crashes for the duration of the day.

Keto meals for women over 50

30+ recipes

1.　Keto Fruits and Veggies for women

Preparation Time: 10 min |Cooking Time: 25 min |Total Time: 35 min

INGREDIENTS:

- 1 Cauliflower
- 1 bell pepper
- 1 cup mushroom slices, fresh
- 1 cup asparagus, chopped
- 1 tbsp. Olive oil

DIRECTIONS:

1. Preheat the oven to 400 ° F (205 ° C). Cover a baking tray with a silicone mat (or foil or baking paper).
2. Cut your cauliflower and bell pepper into equal sized pieces.
3. Slice your mushrooms and chop your asparagus.
4. Drizzle all your vegetables with olive oil.
5. Spread cauliflower, bell pepper, and mushrooms on baking tray. Don't crowd them and leave room for asparagus.
6. Bake for 10 minutes.
7. Stir / turn the vegetables and add asparagus to the pan.
8. Bake for 15 minutes, stir / turn again (after about 7 minutes).
9. Comments
10. The roasting times of vegetables are not 100% reliable. The larger the pieces, the longer it takes to cook.

11. If you want crispier roasted vegetables, shorten the roasting time by a few minutes. If you want softer roasted vegetables, increase the roasting time by up to 10 minutes (except asparagus, which should increase by up to 5 minutes).

2. Napa Cabbage Soup with chicken Meatballs and seafood shrimps

Prep time: 5 min| Cook time: 25 min |Serving 2-4

Ingredients

Soup base

- 2 large slices ginger
- 3 to 4 green onions , chopped
- (Option 1) Quick pork and chicken broth
- 1/4 cup chopped pancetta (or bacon)
- 1 cup chicken stock (or 2 cups, if you want the soup to be extra rich) (Optional)

(Option 2) Clear seafood broth

- 1/4 cup dried shrimp
- 1/4 cup dried scallops
- (Option 3) Easy broth
- 3 cups chicken stock (or pork stock)

Meatballs

- 1/2 pound (230 grams) ground turkey (or ground pork)
- 1/4 cup finely chopped green onion (green part) (Optional)
- 1 tablespoon Shaoxing wine (or dry sherry or Japanese sake)
- 2 teaspoons or tamari for gluten-free
- 2 teaspoons potato starch
- 1 teaspoon ginger , grated
- 1 large egg
- 1/4 teaspoon salt
- 1 teaspoon sesame oil (or peanut oil, or vegetable oil)

Soup base

- 2 enormous cuts ginger
- 3 to 4 green onions , chopped
- (Alternative 1) Quick pork and chicken stock
- 1/4 cup chopped pancetta (or bacon)

- 1 cup chicken stock (or 2 cups, in the event that you need the soup to be additional rich) (Optional)

(Alternative 2) Clear fish stock
- 1/4 cup dried shrimp
- 1/4 cup dried scallops
- (Alternative 3) Easy stock
- 3 cups chicken stock (or pork stock)

Meatballs
- 1/2 pound (230 grams) ground turkey (or ground pork)
- 1/4 cup finely chopped green onion (green part) (Optional)
- 1 tablespoon Shaoxing wine (or dry sherry or Japanese purpose)
- 2 teaspoons or tamari for sans gluten
- 2 teaspoons potato starch
- 1 teaspoon ginger , ground
- 1 huge egg
- 1/4 teaspoon salt
- 1 teaspoon sesame oil (or nut oil, or vegetable oil)

Soup

- 6 to 8 huge napa cabbage leaves , chopped (create 6 to 8 cups)
- 1/2 daikon radish, stripped and chopped (creates 2 cups) (Optional)
- 1 clump enoki mushrooms brilliant needle mushrooms, intense closures eliminated and isolated
- 1/2 (400g/14-ounces) block delicate tofu , chopped
- Ocean salt to taste

Directions

1. Soup base alternative 1 - Quick pork and chicken stock
2. Heat a 3.8-liter (4-quart) pot over medium heat and add the greasy pieces of the pancetta. At the point when it begins to sizzle, go to medium low heat. Blending once in a while, cook until the fat renders and the pancetta becomes brilliant.
3. Add the lean pieces of the pancetta. Keep cooking and blending until brown.
4. Add chicken stock and promptly utilize a spatula to scratch the brown pieces off the

lower part of the pot. Add 2 cups water (add 1 cup water, if using 2 cups chicken stock; or 3 cups water + 1 tablespoon shellfish sauce or hoisin sauce, in the event that you would prefer not to utilize chicken stock), ginger, and green onion. Cook over high heat until bubbling. Go to medium low heat. Cover and bubble for 5 minutes.

Soup base choice 2 - Clear fish stock

5. Flush dried scallops. Spot scallops in a little bowl and add water to cover. Rehydrate for 2 to 3 hours. Channel and attack little pieces.

6. Wash dried shrimp, move to a little bowl, and add water to cover. Rehydrate for 30 minutes. Channel and put in a safe spot.

7. Join the rehydrated scallops and shrimp, ginger, green onion, and 3 cups water in a 3.8-liter (4-quart) pot. Heat over high heat until bubbling. Go to medium heat. Cover and let stew for 5 minutes.

Soup base alternative 3 - Easy stock

8. Join chicken stock (or pork stock), ginger, and green onion in a 3.8-liter (4-quart) pot. Heat over high heat until bubbling. Go to medium heat. Cover and bubble for 5 minutes.

Meatballs

9. Consolidate every one of the ingredients for the meatballs in an enormous bowl. Mix until all ingredients are simply joined and structure a somewhat runny blend. Don't over-mix it. Let sit for 5 to 10 minutes.

Soup:

10. Wash and cut veggies while letting the stock stew.

11. Add daikon radish into the soup pot. Cover and cook for 5 minutes.

12. Add the thick pieces of the napa cabbage. Cover and cook for 5 minutes.

13. Add the green pieces of the napa cabbage and enoki mushroom into the soup. Cook for 2 to 3 minutes.

14. You can change the flavoring now, by adding somewhat salt, if necessary.

15. Add delicate tofu. Push every one of the ingredients aside of the pot, to clear some space for the meatballs. (On the off chance that you need more space in the pot, you can take out a portion of the napa cabbage leaves)

16. Utilize a spoon to scoop 1 to 1.5 tablespoons of the meatball blend and cautiously add it into the soup. Rehash this until you've made around 15 meatballs.

17. Cover the pot and stew until the meatballs are simply cooked through, 4 to 5 minutes. Mood killer heat promptly and eliminate the pot from the oven, keeping it covered.

18. Serve hot as a principle or side. To make it a full dinner, you can heat up certain noodles (or mung bean noodles or shirataki noodles) and add them into the soup toward the finish of cooking. For this situation, you should add a smidgen more salt or light soy sauce, to make the stock somewhat saltier. Thusly, it will taste perfectly with the noodles.

3. Keto Cauliflower bread

Time: 25 MINUTES Cooking time: 50 MINUTES

Total time: 1 HOUR 15 MINUTES

INGREDIENTS:

- 6-tablespoons canola oil (use olive oil if making paleo or keto)
- 1 tbsp. baking powder
- 1-¼ cup of superfine almond flour
- 3 cups of cauliflower finely chopped
- 6-large eggs separated
- 1 tsp. salt

DIRECTIONS:

1. Firstly cook cauliflower for 3-4 minutes or until tender. Let the cauliflower cool. Once cooled, put a small amount in a tea towel and wring dry. Repeat with the remaining cauliflower, working in small batches.

2. Add egg whites to a mixing bowl. Beat at high speed until stiff peaks form. Put aside.

3. In a large bowl, combine egg yolks, oil, almond flour, baking powder, and salt. Mix until smooth paste forms. Stir in the cauliflower until evenly blended.

4. Add about 1/4 of the egg whites to the pasta. Use a spatula to fold in the egg whites. When the egg whites are completely collapsed, add another batch of egg whites and repeat until all of the egg whites have been processed. The mixture should look pale and fluffy. Be careful not to beat the egg whites as they will lose the air that is whipped in, and the bread will not rise properly.

5. Pour the batter into the prepared bread machine. Adjust the program of bread machine. Bake for about 45-50 minutes, or until bread is cooked through. Let the bread cool before slicing.

4.   Chicken Meatballs and Cauliflower Rice with Coconut Herb Sauce

PREP: 25 MIN | COOKING: 20 MIN | TOTAL: 45 MIN | Servings 4

INGREDIENTS:

MEATBALLS

- Non-stick spray
- 1-tablespoon of extra virgin olive oil
- ½ red onion
- 2-cloves of garlic, chopped
- 1 pound of ground chicken
- ¼ cup of chopped fresh parsley
- 1-tablespoon of Dijon mustard
- ¾ teaspoon of kosher salt
- ½ teaspoon of freshly ground black pepper

SAUCE

- A 14-ounce of coconut milk
- 1¼ cups of chopped fresh parsley, divided
- 4-spring onions, roughly chopped
- 1-clove of garlic, peeled and crushed
- Peel and juice one lemon
- Kosher salt and freshly ground black pepper
- Red pepper flakes, to serve
- One recipe Cauliflower rice

DIRECTIONS:

MAKE THE MEATBALLS:

1. Preheat oven to 375 ° F. Line a baking tray with aluminum foil and spray with nonstick cooking spray.

2. In a medium skillet, heat the olive oil over medium heat. Add the onion and sauté until tender, about 5 minutes. Add the garlic and sauté until fragrant, about 1 minute.

3. Transfer the onion and garlic to a medium bowl and allow cooling slightly. Stir in chicken, parsley, and mustard; Season with salt and pepper. Shape the mixture into two tablespoons large balls and place on the baking tray.

4. Fry the meatballs until firm and cooked for 17 to 20 minutes.

MAKE THE SAUCE:

5. In the bowl of a food processor, combine the coconut milk, parsley, spring onions, garlic, lemon zest, and lemon juice and mix until smooth; Season with salt and pepper.

6. Sprinkle the meatballs with the red pepper flakes and the rest of the parsley. Serve over the cauliflower rice with the sauce.

5.   Keto Zucchini Muffins

Prep Time: 10 minutes Cooking Time: 1 hour

Total Time: 1 hour 10 minutes Serves: 12 slices

Calories: 166kcal

INGREDIENTS:

- 2 cups of almond flour (click here to see my favorite on Amazon)
- 1/2 teaspoon Kosher salt
- 1/2 teaspoon ground cinnamon
- 1/2 cup granular sweetener (click here to see my favorite on Amazon)
- 1-teaspoon of baking powder
- 2-large eggs, beaten
- 1/4 cup melted butter
- 1 1/2 cups shredded zucchini with skin

DIRECTIONS:

1. Preheat the oven to 350F. Grease a 9x5 loaf pan with butter or cooking spray.
2. In a large bowl, combine the almond flour, salt, cinnamon, swerve, and baking powder.
3. Wrap the grated zucchini in a tea towel and squeeze out as much liquid as possible. Discard any liquid and add zucchini to the dry, followed by the eggs and melted butter. Stir the batter until combined. See notes for adding walnuts, chocolate chips, or blueberries.
4. Pour the batter into a greased loaf pan and bake in the 350F oven for 60 minutes or until a toothpick comes out clean. Let cool before serving. Cut into 12 slices. See notes for freezing, making muffins, and savory bread.

6.   Best-Ever Guacamole

YIELDS: 6 SERVINGS | PREP TIME: 0 HOURS 10 MINS | TOTAL TIME: 0 HOURS 10 MINS

INGREDIENTS

- 3 avocados, pitted
- Juice of 2 limes
- 1/4 c. freshly chopped cilantro, plus more for garnish
- 1/2 small white onion, finely chopped
- 1 small jalapeño (seeded if you prefer less heat), minced
- 1/2 tsp. kosher salt

DIRECTIONS

1. In a big bowl, mix avocados, lime juice, cilantro, onion, jalapeño and salt.

2. Stir, then slowly turn the bowl as you run a fork through the avocados (this will ensure the mixture stays chunky). Once it's reached your desired thickness, season with more salt if needed. Garnish with more cilantro before serving.

7. Low-Carb Beef Bourguignon Stew

Prep Time 30 minutes | Cook Time 30 minutes

Total Time 1 hour | Servings 6

Ingredients

- 4 slices bacon Sliced crosswise
- 1 1/2 pound stew meat cut into 1 1/2 -2 inch cubes and dried with a paper towel
- 4 ounces white onion (about 1 small)
- 2 stalks celery sliced
- 8 ounces mushrooms thickly sliced
- 1 clove garlic crushed
- 1/2 teaspoon xanthan gum
- 1 cup dry burgundy wine
- 1 cup beef stock (or low-salt broth)
- 2 tablespoons tomato paste

- 1/2 teaspoon dried thyme
- 1 bay leaf
- 1/2 teaspoon sea salt (or to taste)
- 1/4 teaspoon black pepper freshly ground
- 1 tablespoon fresh parsley chopped

Instructions

Instant Pot instructions:

1. With cover off of the Instant Pot, choose the sauté setting. When the "hot" indications shows, add the bacon. Cook bacon, stirring occasionally, until crisp. Remove to a paper towel lined plate. Do not discard bacon grease.

2. Add half of the beef to the Instant Pot. Pieces should not be touching. Drizzle with salt and pepper. Allow the first side brown before turning. Brown all sides and remove to a plate. Repeat for the other half of the meat. If the Instant Pot turns off during this process, set it to Sauté once again.

3. Abandon all but 1 tablespoon of drippings from the pot. (If there is less than 1 tablespoon, add about a tablespoon of butter or preferred oil to the Instant Pot) Continuing on the sauté setting, add onion and celery to the pot. Allow

to cook until just starting to soften. Add mushrooms. Cook vegetables until mushrooms start to soften. Stir in garlic and cook for one minute. Transfer it to a plate

4. If there isn't any oil left in the pot, add about a teaspoon. Add xanthan gum to the pot. Stir to distribute oil through the xanthan gum. Pour in burgundy and stir, scraping up browned bits. Bring to a simmer and simmer until wine starts to condense. Add beef broth. Stir in tomato paste, thyme and bay leaf. Bring to a simmer. Allow to simmer until broth has thickened enough to coat a spoon. Return vegetables browned chunks of beef (along with the drippings), and bacon to the pot. Stir in salt and pepper.

5. Cover Instant Pot. Position steam release handles to "Sealing". Choose the Meat/Stew function and press +/- buttons to adjust time to 30 minutes. When stew is done, use the Quick Release method (consult Instant Pot instruction manual) to vent the Instant Pot. Press Cancel. Be sure the float valve is down before opening the lid.

6. Taste and adjust seasoning. Remove bay leaf and sprinkle with parsley before serving.

7. Slow cooker instructions: (add 5 hours and 30 minutes to cooking time)

8. Heat a large soup pot or Dutch oven over medium high heat. When the pot is hot, add the bacon. Cook bacon, stirring occasionally, until crisp. Remove to a paper towel lined plate to drain then transfer to the slow-cooker

9. Add half of the beef to the pot. Chunks should not be touching. Sprinkle with salt and pepper. Allow the first side brown before turning. Brown all sides then transfer to the slow-cooker. Repeat for the other half of the meat.

10. Discard all but 1 tablespoon of drippings from the pot. If there is less than a tablespoon, add a bit of your choice of oil. Continuing over medium-high heat, add onion and celery to the pot. Allow to cook until just starting to soften. Add mushrooms. Cook vegetables until mushrooms start to soften. Stir in garlic and cook for one minute. Allocate vegetables to the crock pot.

11. If there is no oil left in the pot, add about a teaspoon of oil of your choice. Add xanthan gum to the pot. Stir to divide all in the oil. Pour in burgundy and stir, scraping up browned bits. Bring to a simmer and simmer until wine starts to thicken. Add beef broth. Stir in tomato paste, thyme and bay leaf. Bring to a simmer. Permit to simmer until broth has thickened enough to coat a spoon. Stir in salt and pepper. Transfer to the slow-cooker and stir together with the bacon, beef and the vegetables.

12. Cover the slow-cooker. Cook stew on low 6-8 hours or until meat is fall-apart tender.

13. Before serving, taste and adjust seasoning. Remove bay leaf and drizzle with parsley before serving.

8.   Italian Egg Bake

Preparation time 10 minutes | Cooking time 18 minutes | Total time 28 minutes | Yield 4.5 servings

INGREDIENTS:

- 4 ounces of diced pancetta
- 1/2 cup of chopped red onion (about 140 grams)
- 1/2 cup of chopped fresh oregano
- 1/2 cup of chopped fresh basil
- 1/4 cup of unsweetened almond milk

- 2/3 cup grated Parmesan cheese (extra for topping)
- 1/2 teaspoon of chopped garlic
- 1/4 teaspoon sea salt and pepper each (or to taste)
- 1/2 cup chopped fresh tomato
- 1 cup of tomato sauce
- 5 large cage-free eggs
- Red pepper flakes for garnish
- Oregano for garnish

DIRECTIONS:

1. Preheat the oven to 425 degrees F.
2. Fry the pancetta and onion together in an 8 inch cast iron skillet (or oven safe pan) for 2 minutes or until fragrant.
3. Remove from heat.
4. Beat together the almond milk and parmesan cheese. Reserve extra cheese for the topping.
5. Stir in the garlic, tomato, sea salt / pepper, tomato sauce and herbs.
6. Pour the milk tomato mixture over the cast iron skillet (or ovenproof pan) with the onion and pancetta.

7. Using a spatula, make 5 small slits in the pan (evenly spaced) where you can place the eggs so that the yolk doesn't break. Break 5 eggs on top of each crack. If you find you have an egg with a runny yolk, just mix it through the pan, but then add another egg with a solid yolk. Or discard the runny yolk.

8. Add any extra cheese to the eggs and place the skillet in the oven for 15-18 minutes or until the egg whites are set (the yolk softens) and the corners are brown. Baking times vary depending on the oven and the type of skillet being used.

9. Garnish with Italian parsley and red pepper flakes. To enjoy

9. Coconut Curry Cauliflower Soup with Toasted Pepitas

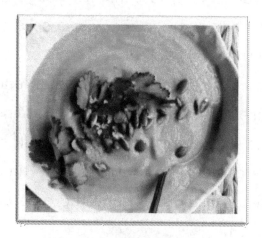

YIELDS: 4

PREP TIME: 0 HOURS 5 MINS

TOTAL TIME: 0 HOURS 35 MINS

INGREDIENTS

- 1/4 c. pepitas, toasted
- 1 tsp. Additional virgin olive oil
- 2 garlic cloves, chopped
- 1 tsp. new ginger, stripped and chopped
- 1 c. yellow onion, chopped
- 1 c. carrots, chopped
- 1 tsp. legitimate salt
- 1 huge cauliflower head, cut into florets

- 32 oz. low-sodium vegetable stock
- 1 c. full-fat coconut milk (shake well ahead of time)
- 2 tbsp. red curry paste
- 1/4 c. new cilantro, chopped
- Flaky ocean salt
- This fixing shopping module is made and kept up by an outsider, and imported onto this page. You might have the option to discover more data about this and comparative substance on their site.

DIRECTIONS

1. In a little skillet, dry toast pepitas on low heat until brilliant brown, around 2 minutes. Put in a safe spot.
2. In an enormous pot over medium-low heat, heat olive oil. Add garlic, ginger, onion, carrots, and salt. Cook for 5 minutes.
3. Add cauliflower, stock, coconut milk, and curry paste. Mix well, heat to the point of boiling, and afterward stew for 20 minutes. Mix with a drenching blender until smooth.

10. Lemon Black Pepper Tuna Salad Recipe

Prep Time: 10 minutes | Cooking Time: 0 minutes | Yield: 1 serving

INGREDIENTS:

- 1/3 cucumber, cut into small cubes
- 1/2 small avocado, cut into small cubes
- 1 teaspoon of lemon juice
- 1 can (100-150 g) of tuna
- 1 tablespoon Paleo mayo (use olive oil for AIP)
- 1 tablespoon mustard (omit for AIP)
- Salt to taste
- Salad greens (optional)
- Black pepper to taste (omit AIP)

DIRECTIONS:

1. Mix the diced cucumber and avocado with the lemon juice.

2. Peel the tuna and mix well with the mayo and mustard.

3. Add the tuna to the avocado and cucumber. Add salt to taste.

4. Prepare the green salads (optional: add olive oil and lemon juice to taste).

5. Place the tuna salad on top of the green lettuce.

6. Sprinkle with black pepper.

11. Keto poached egg recipe on smoked haddock and a bed of spinach

Prep time: 10 minutes |Cooking time: 20 minutes | Yield: 2 servings

INGREDIENTS:

- 2 tablespoons (30 ml) of olive oil for cooking
- 1 shallot, peeled and sliced
- 4 oz. (115 g) baby spinach, stalks
- Salt and pepper , to taste
- 2 fillets of smoked haddock (4 oz. / 115 g each), diced (or use smoked salmon)
- 2 large eggs
- Chives cut to garnish

- 1/3 cup (78 ml) Keto Hollandaise sauce (half the recipe there)

DIRECTIONS:

1. Heat the olive oil in a large saucepan over medium heat and add the shallots. After 30 seconds, add the spinach and stir continuously with a wooden spoon. Cook until the spinach has completely shrunk. Season with salt and pepper and set aside to keep warm.

2. At the same time, bring a pan of water to a boil and add the diced haddock, poaching lightly for 8-10 minutes. Drain and set aside to keep warm.

3. To poach the eggs, bring a pot of water to a boil and then simmer. Crack the eggs one at a time in the water and poach them for 4 minutes, then remove with a slotted spoon and set aside on a paper-lined dish. (Simmer the pan with water as you will need it to make the Hollandaise.)

4. For the Hollandaise sauce, beat the 3 egg yolks with the lemon juice in a bowl that you can easily hold over the pan of boiling water. Continue to beat the mixture while holding the bowl over the heat of the boiling water, keeping a close eye on the heat to prevent the eggs from scrambling. Once light and fluffy, add the melted ghee to the eggs 1 tablespoon at a time, whisking continuously until the ghee is completely absorbed and the Hollandaise has thickened.

5. Before serving, divide the warm spinach between two plates and add the diced haddock. Cover with the poached egg and serve with the hollandaise sauce scooped over.

12. Easy Keto Beef Broccoli

Prep Time: 10 minutes | Cook Time: 25 minutes | Total Time: 35 minutes Servings: Servings Calories: 294kcal

Ingredients

- 1 pound flank steak sliced into 1/4 inch thick strips
- 5 cups small broccoli florets about 7 ounces
- 1 tablespoon avocado oil
- For the sauce:
- 1 yellow onion sliced
- 1 Tbsp. butter
- ½ tbsp. olive oil
- 1/3 cup low-sodium soy sauce
- ⅓ cup beef stock

- 1 tablespoon fresh ginger minced
- 2 cloves garlic minced

Instructions

1. Firstly heat avocado oil in a pan over medium heat for a few minutes or until hot.

2. Then add sliced beef and cook until it browns, less than 5 minutes, don't stir too much, you want it to brown. Transfer to a plate and set aside.

3. Add onions to a skillet with butter and olive oil and cook 20 minutes until onions are caramelized and tender.

4. Add all other sauce ingredients into the pan and stir the ingredients together over medium-low heat until it starts to simmer, about 5 minutes.

5. Use an absorption blender to blend sauce.

6. Keep the sauce warm over low heat, and add broccoli to the skillet.

7. Then return beef to the pan and toss with broccoli and sauce top. Stir until everything is coated with the sauce.

8. Bring to a simmer and cook for another few minutes until broccoli is tender.
9. Garnish with salt and pepper to taste, if needed.
10. Serve immediately, optionally pairing with cooked cauliflower rice.

13. Pistachio Crusted Rack of Lamb

Prep: 10 min | Cook: 35 min | Additional: 10 min | Total: 55 min | Servings: 4 | Yield: 4 servings

Ingredients

- 2 racks of lamb, trimmed
- 1 teaspoon herbes de Provence
- salt and ground black pepper to taste
- 1 tablespoon vegetable oil
- ⅔ cup chopped pistachio nuts
- 2 tablespoons dry bread crumbs
- 1 tablespoon melted butter
- 1 teaspoon olive oil
- salt and ground black pepper to taste
- 3 tablespoons Dijon mustard

Directions
Step 1

1. Firstly preheat oven to 400 degrees F (200 degrees C). Line a baking sheet with aluminum foil. Generously season each stand of lamb with herbes de Provence, salt, and black pepper.

Step 2

2. Heat oil in a large pan over high heat. Place lamb in skillet and cook, browning on all sides, 6 to 8 minutes. Transfer lamb to a foil-lined baking sheet; set aside.

Step 3

3. Stir pistachios, bread crumbs, butter, olive oil, and a pinch of salt and black pepper in a bowl. Spread mustard on the fat-side of each holder of lamb. Pat pistachio mixture on top of mustard. Bake in the preheated oven until the crunch is golden and lamb is pink in the center, 20 to 25 minutes. Transfer to a plate and let rest 10 minutes.

14. Asparagus With Hollandaise Sauce (Brown Butter)

Prep Time: 10 minutes | Cook Time: 5 minutes | Total Time: 15 minutes | Servings: 4 Calories: 248kcal

Ingredients

- 1 pound asparagus, trimmed
- 1 tablespoon water
- salt and pepper to taste
- Hollandaise Sauce
- 4 ounces salted butter
- 2 large egg yolks
- 1/2 teaspoon Dijon mustard
- 1 tablespoon water
- 1-2 teaspoons freshly squeezed lemon juice (or white vinegar)

- 1-2 pinch cayenne pepper
- 1-2 pinch white pepper

Instructions

Preparation:

1. If the asparagus is medium to large in wideness, cut 1 inch off of the bottoms and lightly peel the stalks with a vegetable peeler. I start about 1/3 from the top and continue to the bottom of each spear. If the asparagus is thin, hold a spike towards the bottom and bend it until it snaps. Cut the remaining spears to the same length. Discrete the eggs, reserving the whites for another use.

2. Asparagus:

3. Put the asparagus in a microwave safe bowl and add 1 tablespoon of water. Cover with plastic wrap and cook at high power from 1 1/2 - 2 1/2 minutes depending on your microwave. Drain off the water and keep covered. Alternately, blanch the asparagus in boiling water until it is crunchy tender, drain, and keep warm.

4. Blender Hollandaise

5. Add the egg yolks, 1 tablespoon of water, 1 teaspoon of lemon juice and the mustard to a blender. Place the lid on top and remove the middle piece. Place the butter in a medium to large frying pan and melt the butter over medium heat. Turn the heat up to medium high and slightly swirl the pan every few moments. When the solids in the bottom of the pan just begin to turn brown, turn off the heat. Turn the blender on low and begin pouring the hot butter into the blender, leaving the brown solids behind in the pan.

6. After the butter has been incorporated, add the cayenne pepper and white pepper and blend. Taste. Adjust seasoning with more acid, salt or pepper. Pour over the asparagus and serve immediately. Serves 4.

15. Keemacurry

Yield: Serves 4 Prep Time: 10 Minutes Cook Time: 40 Minutes Total Time: 50 Minutes

INGREDIENTS

- 450g (1lb) of extra lean beef mince
- 1 large onion, chopped finely
- 1 large carrot, finely chopped
- 1 stalk of celery, finely chopped
- 3 cloves of garlic, crushed
- 1 heaped teaspoon of fresh grated ginger
- 2 teaspoons of cumin seeds
- 2 teaspoon of ground coriander
- 1 teaspoon of deggi mirch Chilli Powder (can add more if you like it really spicy).
- 1 teaspoon of garam masala
- 1 teaspoon of turmeric
- 1 cup of frozen peas

- 4 tablespoons of tomato paste
- cups (600ml) of beef stock (use just 1.5 cups for instant pot)
- freshly chopped coriander to serve
- salt and black pepper
- cooking oil spray (I used avocado)

INSTRUCTIONS

Stove Top:

1. Spray a frying pan over a medium heat with some spray oil
2. Add the onion, garlic, carrot, celery and ginger and cook for approx 5 mins to soften.
3. Add the minced beef and cook until browned, breaking up large pieces with the back of a wooden ladle while it cooks.
4. Stir in all the spices (plus the green chilli's if using) and tomato paste and mix to evenly coat.
5. Add the stock and bring to a boil, then reduce heat to a simmer until meat is cooked through and stock has reduced to a thicker consistency – approx 30mins
6. Stir in the peas at the last few minutes.

7. Taste and season as needed with salt and black pepper.

8. Serve topped with freshly chopped coriander and steamed rice.

Instant Pot:

9. Set instant pot to sauté mode

10. Add ground beef, onion, celery, carrot, garlic and ginger

11. Fry till beef is browned.

12. Add all other ingredients (expect peas and coriander)

13. Switch to 12 minutes (high) and ensure valve is closed.

14. When it honks to signal it has done cooking, open the valve to quickly release the pressure.

15. Switch to sauté mode again and simmer for about 1-2 mins just to heat through the peas.

16. Taste and season as needed with salt and black pepper.

17. Serve with chopped fresh coriander and your choice of sides.

16. Keto Breakfast Burritos

PREPARATION: 20 minutes COOKING TIME: 10 min TOTAL TIME: 30 min YIELD: 6 SERVINGS

INGREDIENTS:

- 6 strips of bacon cut in the middle
- 10 large eggs, beaten
- 4 spring onions, chopped
- 1/2 red bell pepper, diced
- 1/2 teaspoon of salt
- 12 tablespoons of grated cheddar or pepper jack cheese
- 6 8-inch low-carb flour tortillas (I used Ole Xtreme Wellness)

- 6 pieces Reynolds Wrap Heavy-Duty Aluminum Foil , cut 25 x 30 cm each
- hot sauce for serving, optional

DIRECTIONS:

1. Cook both sides of the tortillas on a hot baking tray or over an open flame. Keep it warm in the oven if you eat right away. This helps the tortillas get smoother and also improves the flavor in my opinion.
2. Heat a large non-stick frying pan over medium heat. Add the bacon and cook until cooked through, about 4 to 5 minutes. Transfer with a slotted spoon to drain onto a paper towel-lined plate.
3. Beat the eggs with salt in a large bowl. Stir in the spring onions and bell pepper.
4. Discard the bacon fat and let stand 1 teaspoon and add the eggs, let them rest on the bottom and stir several times to cook through, set aside.
5. On a clean work surface, spread a generous 1/2 cup of the egg mixture over the bottom third of the tortilla. Top each with a slice of bacon and 2 tablespoons of cheese. Roll from

the bottom, fold the left and right corners towards the center and continue to roll into a tight cylinder. Set aside, seam down, and repeat with remaining tortillas and filling.

6. If you want to eat right away, heat a skillet over medium heat. While hot, spray the pan with oil and add the burritos seam side down. Cook, covered, until the bottom of the burritos is golden brown, about 2 minutes on each side. Serve with hot sauce or salsa, if desired.

17. Avocado Crab Boats

Prep/Total Time: 20 min. | Makes: 8 servings

Ingredients

- 5 medium ready avocados, stripped and divided
- 1/2 cup mayonnaise
- 2 tablespoons lemon juice
- 2 jars (6 ounces each) bump crabmeat, depleted
- 4 tablespoons chopped new cilantro, separated
- 2 tablespoons minced chives
- 1 serrano pepper, cultivated and minced
- 1 tablespoon tricks, depleted
- 1/4 teaspoon pepper
- 1 cup shredded pepper jack cheddar
- 1/2 teaspoon paprika
- Lemon wedges

Directions

1. Preheat oven. Spot 2 avocado parts in a large bowl; pound delicately with a fork. Add mayonnaise and lemon juice; blend until very much mixed. Mix in crab, 3 tablespoons cilantro, chives, serrano pepper, tricks and pepper. Spoon into staying avocado parts.

2. Move to a 15x10x1-in. heating container. Sprinkle with cheddar and paprika. Sear 4-5 in. from heat until cheddar is dissolved, 3-5 minutes. Sprinkle with residual cilantro; present with lemon wedges.

18. Keto meat pie

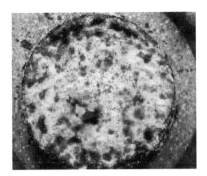

30 minutes preparation| 40 minutes cooking time| 6 servings

Ingredients

Meat filling

- ½ (2 oz.) yellow onion, finely chopped
- 1 garlic clove, finely chopped
- 2 tbsp. butter or olive oil
- 1¼ lbs. ground beef or ground turkey
- 2 tbsp. dried oregano or dried basil
- ½ tsp. salt
- ¼ tsp. ground black pepper
- 3 tbsp. tomato paste
- ½ cup water

Pie crust

- ¾ cup (3 oz.) almond flour
- ¼ cup (1¼ oz.) sesame seeds
- ¼ cup (¾ oz.) coconut flour

- 1 tbsp. ground psyllium husk powder
- 1 tsp. baking powder
- 1 pinch salt
- 3 tbsp. olive oil
- 1 large egg
- ¼ cup water

Topping

- 1 cup (7½ oz.) cottage cheese
- 1 cup (4 oz.) cheddar cheese, shredded

Instructions

Meat filling

1. Firstly preheat the oven to 350°F (175°C).
2. Heat the butter or olive oil in a big frying pan, over medium heat. Add the onion and cook for a few minutes until tender. Add the garlic, ground beef, oregano or basil, salt, and pepper. Use a spatula to break the meat into smaller pieces, while mixing together. Cook for 8-10 minutes or until no longer pink.
3. Add the tomato paste, water, and stir to mix. Reduce heat to medium-low, and simmer uncovered for 20 minutes, stirring infrequently. Meanwhile, prepare the pie crust.

Pie crust

4. Combine the crust ingredients together using a food processor, or with a fork.

5. Place a round piece of parchment paper in a well-greased, 9-10" (23-25 cm) spring form pan, or deep-dish pie pan. Using a spatula or well-greased fingers, evenly press the dough onto the base and the sides of the pan. Pierce the base and sides of the crust with a fork, to prevent bubbling.

6. Pre-bake the crust for 10 minutes. Remove from the oven and place the meat mixture in the crust.

7. In a little bowl, mix the cottage cheese and shredded cheese. Spread on top of the pie.

8. Bake on the lower rack for 30-40 minutes, or until golden in color.

19. Keto Long Noodle Soup

Prep/Total Time: 30 min.| Makes: 6 servings (2 quarts

Ingredients

- 6 ounces uncooked Asian lo Mein noodles
- 1 pork tenderloin (3/4 pound), cut into meager strips
- 2 tablespoons soy sauce, isolated
- 1/8 teaspoon pepper
- 2 tablespoons canola oil, isolated
- 1-1/2 teaspoons minced new gingerroot
- 1 garlic clove, minced
- 1 container (32 ounces) chicken stock

- 1 celery rib, meagerly cut
- 1 cup new snow peas, divided corner to corner
- 1 cup coleslaw blend
- 2 green onions, cut askew
- New cilantro leaves, discretionary

Directions

1. Cook noodles as per bundle directions. Channel and flush with cold water; channel well.

2. Then, throw pork with 1 tablespoon soy sauce and pepper. In a 6-qt. stockpot, heat 1 tablespoon oil over medium-high heat; sauté pork until delicately browned, 2-3 minutes. Eliminate from pot.

3. In same pot, heat remaining oil over medium-high heat; sauté ginger and garlic until fragrant, 20-30 seconds. Mix in stock and remaining soy sauce; heat to the point of boiling. Add celery and snow peas; get back to a bubble. Stew, revealed, until fresh delicate, 2-3 minutes. Mix in pork and coleslaw blend; cook just until cabbage starts to shrink. Add noodles; eliminate from heat. Top with green onions and, whenever wanted, cilantro.

20. Keto low carb Pumpkin Pie

Yield: 16 Servings | Prep Time: 0 Hours 15 Min | Total Time: 3 Hours 30 Min

INGREDIENTS:

FOR THE CRUST

- 1 1/2 c. almond flour
- 3 tablespoons. coconut flour
- 1/4 tsp. baking powder
- 1/4 tsp. kosher salt
- 4 tbsp. melted butter
- 1 large egg, beaten

BEFORE FILLING

- 1 (15-oz.) Can pumpkin puree
- 1 c. heavy cream
- 1/2 c. packaged keto-friendly brown sugar, such as Swerve
- 3 large eggs, beaten
- 1 tsp. ground cinnamon
- 1/2 tsp. ground ginger
- 1/4 tsp. ground nutmeg
- 1/4 tsp. ground cloves
- 1/4 tsp. kosher salt
- 1 tsp. pure vanilla extract
- Whipped cream, to serve (optional)

DIRECTIONS

1. Preheat the oven to 350 °. In a large bowl, combine almond flour, coconut flour, baking powder, and salt. Add the melted butter and the egg and stir until a dough form. Press the dough evenly into a 23 cm cake plate and poke holes all over the crust with a fork.
2. Bake lightly golden brown for 10 minutes.
3. In a large bowl, beat pumpkin, cream, brown sugar, eggs, spices, and vanilla until smooth.

Pour the pumpkin mixture into pre-baked crust.

4. Bake until the filling wobbles slightly in the center and the crust is golden brown, 45 to 50 minutes.

5. Turn off the oven and open the door. Let the pie cool in the oven for 1 hour, then refrigerate until ready to serve.

6. Serve with whipped cream if desired.

21. Keto Avocado Fudge Cookies

Prep time: 5 minutes | Resting time: 5 minutes | C ALSO time: 12 minutes

INGREDIENTS:

- 100 grams of ripe avocado
- 1 large egg
- 1/2 cup of unsweetened cocoa powder
- 1/4 cup unsweetened shredded coconut
- 1/4 cup of erythritol
- 1/2 teaspoon of baking powder
- 3/8 tsp. liquid stevia
- 1/4 teaspoon of pink Himalayan salt

DIRECTIONS:

1. Preheat your oven to 350 degrees F and line a baking sheet with parchment paper.

2. Cut the avocado into the skin and place it in a large mixing bowl. Puree as much as possible with a fork.

3. Add the egg, erythritol, stevia and salt and mix with a hand mixer to a uniform consistency.

4. Add the cocoa, coconut flakes and baking powder and mix again.

5. Scoop 9 cookies onto the baking tray with a cookie scoop. Use a spoon or your finger to spread the cookies out to the desired size.

6. Optionally, cover with lily of chocolate or abraded baker chocolate. Bake for 10-12 minutes, until set.

7. Let cool for five minutes before using.

8. Best store in a zip-lock bag in the refrigerator for up to a week. To enjoy!

22. Keto Breaded fish recipe (with cod)

Prep time: 10 minutes | Cooking time: 20 minutes | Yield: 4 servings

INGREDIENTS:

- 4 cod fillets (about 0.3 lb. each) (or use other fish)
- 1/2 cup of coconut flour
- 2 tablespoons of coconut flakes
- 3 tablespoons of garlic powder
- 1 tablespoon of onion powder
- Salt to taste
- 2 tablespoons of ghee
- 3 cloves of garlic, chopped
- Coconut oil for greasing baking tray

DIRECTIONS:

1. Preheat the oven to 425F (220C).
2. In a large bowl, combine the breading (coconut flour, coconut flakes, garlic powder, and onion powder). Add salt and taste the mixture to see how much salt you like.
3. Cover a baking tray with aluminum foil and grease with coconut oil .
4. Dip each fish fillet in the breading mixture and cover well. Place the breaded fish on the baking tray.
5. Bake for 15-20 minutes until the fish flakes easily.
6. While the fish is in the oven, prepare the garlic ghee sauce by melting the ghee a little and adding the chopped garlic.
7. Pour the garlic ghee sauce over the breaded fish and serve.

23. Keto Low Carb Oven Baked Fish

Preparation Time: 25 mins |Cooking Time: 20 mins |Total Time: 45 mins | Servings: 4

INGREDIENTS:

- For breading
- For the eggs
- For the fish
- For the pan

DIRECTIONS:

1. To Prepare: Preheat the oven to 430 ° F. Add a dark colored pan or baking tray to the oven while it heats up - the pan you want to bake the fish in must be hot to melt the butter!

2. Making breadcrumbs: Mix all of them for the breading in a shallow bowl.

3. Preparing eggs: Add the eggs to a SEPARATE shallow dish and beat well.

4. Bread fish: Dip the fish in breadcrumbs to lightly coat it. Then cover the fish with egg. FINALLY, cover the fish with breadcrumbs again, this time you can really grab as much as it sticks! (Just put the breaded pieces of fish on a plate until you've breaded them all.)

5. Melting butter: Take the pan out of the oven VERY CAREFULLY. Add 3 tablespoons of butter to the pan to melt. Divide over the pan and place the pieces of fish on top.

6. Baking: fry the fish for 10 minutes. Flip, add remaining 1 tablespoon butter and cook for 5-10 minutes or until coating are crisp and fish is cooked through.

7. Finish: grill for 2 minutes for a crispy coating. After cooking, let the fish rest on the pan for 2-3 minutes and serve immediately.

24. Easy Keto Hamburger Casserole Recipe

Prep Time: 15 min| Cook Time: 30 min| Total Time: 45 min

Ingredients

- 1½ pounds ground beef see tips below
- 2 tablespoons olive oil plus more for the pan
- 1 teaspoon onion powder
- 1 teaspoon garlic powder
- 1 teaspoon Dijon mustard
- 1 tablespoon tomato paste sugar-free – see tips below
- ½ teaspoon ground pepper
- 1 teaspoon salt
- 3 eggs
- ½ cup heavy cream
- 1½ cups cheddar grated

- 3 cups green beans canned or frozen – see tips below

Instructions

1. Oil an 8×8" baking dish with olive oil and set aside. Preheat your oven to 360°F. Put 1½ pounds ground beef, 1 teaspoon onion powder, 1 teaspoon garlic powder, 1 teaspoon Dijon mustard, 1 tablespoon tomato paste, ½ teaspoon ground pepper, and 1 teaspoon salt in a large bowl. Stir well until mixed.

2. Ground beef and other ingredients in a glass bowl for keto hamburger casserole

3. Heat 2 tablespoons olive oil in a large skillet. Add the ground beef paste and cook for about 10 minutes, breaking it up as it cooks, until it browns completely.

4. Browning the ground beef in a skillet

5. Add the cooked ground beef mixture to your prepared baking dish in an even layer. Blowout 3 cups canned or frozen green beans over the beef.

6. Green beans on top of beef for keto casserole recipe

7. In a medium bowl, beat 3 eggs. Add ½ cup heavy cream and a pinch of salt. Evenly pour this mixture over the meat and green beans. Spread 1½ cups grated cheese over the top of the beef and green bean mixture.

8. Adding cheese to keto casserole recipe

9. Then bake for 20-30 minutes, until the cheese is golden brown. Present, and enjoy!

10. Serving of keto casserole recipe on a plate with a baking dish of hamburger casserole

Notes

11. Mix with ground pork: You can use ground pork in addition to beef for even more flavor. Use a mixture of 1 pound ground beef and 5 ounces ground pork if you would like to use pork.

12. Sugar-free tomato paste: Make sure your tomato paste is sugar-free. You can substitute it with sugar-free ketchup.

13. Using frozen green beans: If using frozen green beans, you do not need to thaw them. They will cook completely when baking the casserole.

14. Other veggies to use: Not a fan of green beans? You can still make this easy keto hamburger recipe! Try using cauliflower or broccoli instead. Broccoli is one of our personal favorites!

25. Keto Curry Bowl With Spinach

Prep Time: 5 minutes| Cook Time: 10 minutes|
Total Time: 15 minutes\ Servings: 4 NET carbs:
4g

Ingredients

- 1 onion sliced
- 2 cloves garlic
- 2 tbsp. curry powder
- 750 g (1.7 lb.) ground/minced beef
- 125 ml (0.5 cups) coconut cream
- 6 cups spinach chopped finely

Instructions

1. Slightly fry the sliced onion in coconut oil until the onion is cooked and clear.

2. Then add the garlic and curry powder, stir and cook for another minute. Be careful not to allow the garlic to burn.

3. Add the ground/minced beef and endure to stir until thoroughly cooked.

4. Add the coconut cream and stir.

5. At the same time as the curried beef is still simmering in the pan, begin to add the chopped spinach one handful at a time. Stir the spinach through the curried beef so it wilts. Repeat until all the spinach is added.

6. Present the keto curry in bowls, and enjoy! Garnish with coconut cream (optional).

26. Keto Parmesan Roasted Broccoli

Prep/Total Time: 30 min. | makes: 4 servings

Ingredients

- 2 little broccoli crowns (around 8 ounces each)
- 3 tablespoons olive oil
- 1/2 teaspoon salt
- 1/2 teaspoon pepper
- 1/4 teaspoon squashed red pepper chips
- 4 garlic cloves, daintily cut
- 2 tablespoons ground Parmesan cheddar
- 1 teaspoon ground lemon zing

Directions

1. Preheat oven to 425°. Cut broccoli crowns into quarters through and through. Shower with oil; sprinkle with salt, pepper and pepper drops. Spot in a material lined 15x10x1-in. skillet.

2. Broil until fresh delicate, 10-12 minutes. Sprinkle with garlic; cook 5 minutes longer. Sprinkle with cheddar; broil until cheddar is dissolved and stalks of broccoli are delicate, 2-4 minutes more. Sprinkle with lemon zing.

Nutrition Facts

- 2 broccoli pieces:
- 144 calories
- 11g fat (2g saturated fat)
- 2mg cholesterol
- 378mg sodium
- 9g carbohydrate (2g sugars, 3g fiber)
- 4g protein
- Diabetic Exchanges: 2 fat
- 1 vegetable

27. Keto Spicy Pork Brussels Bowls

PREP TIME: 5 min | COOK TIME: 25 min |

TOTAL TIME: 30 min | YIELD: 4 SERVINGS |

COURSE: Dinner, Lunch, Meal Prep

INGREDIENTS

- olive oil spray
- 1 pound 90% lean ground pork, or swap it for a meatless ground meat option
- 2 tablespoons red wine vinegar
- 3 cloves garlic, minced
- 1 teaspoon smoky paprika
- 2 teaspoons ancho chili powder
- 1 teaspoon kosher salt
- 1/4 teaspoon cayenne pepper
- 1/4 teaspoon freshly ground black pepper
- 1/4 teaspoon dried oregano

- 1/4 teaspoon ground cumin
- 6 cups shredded brussels sprouts
- 1/4 cup chopped onion
- 4 large eggs

INSTRUCTIONS

1. Heat a large cast iron or heavy nonstick skillet over medium heat, spray with oil and cook the meat, breaking it up in small pieces.
2. Combine spices in a small bowl.
3. spices
4. Add garlic, season with spices and vinegar and cook until browned and no longer pink in the middle, 8 to 10 minutes.
5. ground pork in a skillet
6. Set it aside on a plate.
7. Add the brussels and onions to the pan and cook over high heat, stirring occasionally until the brussels start to brown and are tender crisp, 6 to 7 minutes.
8. Return the pork to the skillet and mix everything together 1 to 2 minutes.
9. Heat a nonstick skillet or pan and spray with oil, when hot cook the eggs, covered until the

whites are just set and the yolks are still runny, 2 to 3 minutes.

28. Keto Creamy Cauliflower Vegetable Soup

Cooking Time: 20 mins |Total Time: 25 mins |

Servings: 32 bites | Calories: 337kcal

INGREDIENTS:

- 1 pound of cauliflower
- 1 cup of heavy cream
- 2 teaspoons of Salt
- 1 teaspoon pepper white, ground
- 1/2 teaspoon ground nutmeg
- 2 oz. butter salted

DIRECTIONS:

1. Cut the cauliflower into even sized pieces and put them in a pan

2. Add the whipped cream to the pan and fill the pan with water until only the tips of the cauliflower are above the water.

3. Bring the cauliflower to a boil and simmer for 10 minutes, until very tender and break apart easily with a spoon.

4. Add salt, pepper, nutmeg and butter.

5. Mix the soup with a hand blender, being careful not to splash yourself with the hot liquid. We recommend mixing in short bursts until the mixture is smooth.

6. Spoon the soup into 4 bowls to serve and enjoy.

29. Keto Soft Pretzels Recipe - The original low-carb version, delicious!

INGREDIENTS:

- 2-teaspoons of dried yeast
- 1-teaspoon of inulin
- 2-tablespoons of warm water
- 5.5 grams of almond flour
- 2-teaspoons of Xanthan gum
- 11 ounces of mozzarella cheese shredded
- 4-tablespoons of cream cheese
- 2-large eggs at room temperature
- 2-tablespoons of salted butter melted
- 1-tablespoon pretzel salt flakes sea salt can be substituted

DIRECTIONS:

1. Preheat the oven to 200C / 390F. Place the yeast, inulin, and warm water in a bowl. Mix well and let rise for 5 minutes. In a large mixing bowl, add the almond flour and xanthan gum.

2. Mix well and set aside. Place a non-stick pan over medium heat and add the mozzarella and cream cheese. Keep a close eye on it as it melts and frequently stirs to avoid browning.

3. Heat until the cheese is thick and pourable. Add the aged yeast and the melted cheese to the almond flour, mix 1 minute before adding the eggs.

4. Mix until a smooth and sticky dough is formed. I recommend putting on food-safe gloves and mixing by hand. Let rest for 5 minutes to rest.

5. Divide the dough into quarters and each quarter into three pieces so that you have 12 balls. The dough is easiest to handle when it is warm and with food-safe gloves.

6. Roll each ball into a long thin block and twist into a pretzel shape. Place them on a

parchment-lined baking tray and give a little space with the side as the pretzels will rise.

7. Sprinkle the pretzels with the butter and sprinkle with salt. Bake in the oven for 12-15 minutes. When the pretzels are golden brown, remove them from the oven.

8. Do not burn your fingers if you try to eat them immediately. Let them cool for 5 minutes before enjoying.

30. Keto Wonton Soup with shrimps

Prep Time: 1 HOUR | Cook Time: 5 MINUTES | Total Time: 1 HOUR 5 MINUTES | Servings: 8 servings

Ingredients

- 1 pack wonton coverings (80 coverings)
- Filling
- 1/2 lbs. (230 g) ground lean pork
- 1/2 lbs. (230 g) stripped shrimp, chopped into little pieces
- 1 tablespoon finely minced ginger
- 2 green onions , finely chopped

- 1 tablespoon light soy sauce (or soy sauce)
- 2 tablespoons Shaoxing wine (or dry sherry)
- 1/2 teaspoon salt
- 2 tablespoons sesame oil
- (Alternative 1) Chicken soup base
- 8 cups chicken stock
- 8 teaspoons light soy sauce (or soy sauce)
- 8 teaspoons minced ginger
- 8 teaspoons sesame oil
- Salt, to taste
- (Choice 2) Chinese road style soup base
- 8 cups hot stock from the wonton bubbling water
- 8 tablespoons papery dried shrimp, or to taste
- 8 major bits of dried ocean growth for soup, arranged by guidance.
- 4 teaspoons chicken bouillon
- 8 teaspoons light soy sauce , or to taste
- 8 teaspoons sesame oil
- Garnishes
- 4 green onions , chopped
- 4 stalks infant bok choy , slice to reduced down (or 4 cups infant spinach)
- 1 bunch cilantro, chopped (Optional)
- Hand crafted stew oil , to taste (Optional)

Directions
Make the filling

1. Without a food processor: Combine ground pork, shrimp, ginger, green onion, soy sauce, Shaoxing wine, salt and sesame oil in a major bowl. Blend well in with a fork until everything consolidates well together and the combination feels somewhat tacky.

2. With a food processor or a blender: coarsely cleave the ginger and green onion. Add all the filling ingredients with the exception of the shrimp. Blend until it frames a velvety paste. Add the shrimp and mix once more, until the shrimp are finely chopped however don't turn into a paste.

3. Wrap the wonton

To make wontons

4. Place a wonton covering in one hand, scoop a teaspoon of wonton filling and spot it close to the restricted side of the wonton covering (you can add more filling to the wonton on the off chance that you like, as long as you can in any case wrap it).

5. Overlap the restricted side over the filling; at that point roll the filling right through the opposite side of the covering. Tie the two finishes and press together to bolt the filling inside the covering. Brush a dainty layer of water onto the wonton covering and press the closures together.

6. Make each wonton in turn, and line up every one of the wontons on a major wooden cutting board. In the event that you're not going to heat up the wontons promptly, utilize a moist paper towel (or cheesecloth) to cover the wontons to keep them from drying out.

7. On the off chance that you're not going to heat up the wontons that very day, place them in a water/air proof holder with a few layers of wet paper towels on the base. Thusly, they can be put away in the cooler for as long as 2 days.

(Alternative 1) Make the chicken soup base

8. Consolidate the chicken stock, ginger, and soy sauce in a pot. Heat to the point of boiling. Let bubble for 10 minutes. Go to least heat to keep warm and begin cooking wontons (see beneath).

9. Plan 8 medium-sized dishes. Add the cooked wontons and bok choy. Add 2 tablespoons green onion, 1 tablespoon soy sauce and 1/2 teaspoon sesame oil into each bowl. Pour in 1 and 1/2 cups hot stock. Trimming with cilantro and stew oil, if using.

10. Serve hot.

(Alternative 2) Make the road seller style soup base

11. To get ready 1 serving of wonton soup base, add a major spoon of cilantro, 1 tablespoon papery dried shrimps, a liberal piece of dried kelp, 1/4 teaspoon chicken bouillon, and some child bok choy into a major bowl. Rehash the interaction to set up the remainder of the soup base in the other serving bowls. Cook wontons (see beneath).

12. To make 1 serving of wonton soup, utilize a spoon to move cooked wontons, bok choy, and the hot soup into a serving bowl with every one of the ingredients from the past advance. Sprinkle 1 teaspoon soy sauce and 1 teaspoon sesame oil into the bowl and give it a delicate mix. The soup ought to be golden hued. Add

additional soy sauce or salt if the soup isn't sufficiently pungent. Dissipate green onion on top. Enhancement with cilantro and stew oil, if using.

13. Serve hot.

Heated up the wonton

14. To heat up the wontons, heat a major pot of water until bubbling. Add 10 to 20 wontons all at once and bubble over medium heat until wontons are drifting on the outside of the water.

15. Keep on bubbling until the coverings are swollen, around 1 to 2 minutes for little wontons and 2 to 3 minutes for greater ones. Take a wonton out with an opened spoon and split it with a chopstick or fork. On the off chance that the wonton is cooked through, stop heat quickly and move the wontons to singular serving bowls. If not, keep on bubbling until cooked through.

16. Whenever you've cooked the wontons, add the bok choy. Let cook until delicate. Eliminate from the pot, channel well, and put in a safe spot.

To cook frozen wontons

17. Heat a huge pot of water to the point of boiling over high heat. Add wontons. Mix tenderly to keep from staying.

18. Cook until heating the water to the point of boiling once more. Go to medium-low heat. Cover the pot with a little hole on one side, to forestall spilling. Keep bubbling for 2 minutes (3 minutes for bigger wontons). Remain adjacent to the pot the entire chance to screen the stock.

19. On the off chance that the stock begins to spill, reveal and mix, and supplant the cover. Uncover and keep cooking for one more moment, or until the wontons are cooked through.

20. There are numerous kinds of dried ocean growth. My unique formula utilized a sort of moment ocean growth that will rehydrate quickly once positioned into the hot soup. There are different kinds of fish that require some splashing prior to using. Peruse the rear of your bundle and adhere to the guidelines as needs be.

21. The sustenance realities for this formula are determined dependent on 1 bowl of chicken-stock based soup containing 10 wontons.

31. Keto Salmon Curry

Prep Time: 10 minutes | Cooking Time: 15 minutes | Yield: 2 servings

DIRECTIONS:

- 1/2 medium onion, diced or finely chopped
- 2 cups (7 oz. or 200 g) green beans, diced
- 1.5 tablespoons (10 g) of curry powder
- 1 teaspoon (3 g) of garlic powder
- Cream the top of 1 (14-oz) can of coconut milk
- 2 cups (480 ml) of bone broth
- 1 lb. (450 g) raw salmon, diced (defrost first if frozen)
- 2 tablespoons (30 ml) of coconut oil for cooking

- Salt and pepper , to taste
- 2 tablespoons of basil (4 g), chopped, for garnish

DIRECTIONS:

1. Cook the diced onion in the coconut oil until translucent.
2. Add the green beans and cook for a few more minutes.
3. Add the stock or water and bring to the boil.
4. Add the curry powder, garlic powder and salmon.
5. Add the coconut cream and simmer until the salmon is tender (3-5 minutes).
6. Add salt and pepper to taste and serve with the chopped basil.

32. Keto Tomato Tuna Bruschetta Recipe

Prep time: 10 minutes | Cooking time: 5 minutes | Yield: 4 servings

INGREDIENTS:

- 4 slices of Keto bread
- 4 tablespoons (60 ml) of olive oil
- 1 6oz (170 g) canned tuna , drained and flaked
- 1 tomato, seeded and cut into small cubes
- 1 tablespoon (15 ml) lemon juice
- 1/4 cup parsley, chopped
- Salt and pepper , to taste

DIRECTIONS:

1. Toast 4 slices of keto bread.

2. Divide the olive oil over the slices of toast.

3. In a small bowl, combine the tuna, tomato, lemon juice, and parsley. Season with salt and pepper.

4. Drizzle with extra olive oil, if desired.

Conclusion

I would like to thank you all for going through this book. All the recipes in this book are for women over 50 who want to have low carb meals and especially for beginners. All recipes are very easy to take a start with Try these dishes at home and appreciate. Wish you good luck!

CPSIA information can be obtained
at www.ICGtesting.com
Printed in the USA
LVHW051101010621
689026LV00008B/1089